C000170635

BRITAIN IN OLD PHOTOGRAPHS

BLETCHLEY

ROBERT COOK

ALAN SUTTON PUBLISHING LIMITED

Alan Sutton Publishing Limited
Phoenix Mill · Far Thrupp · Stroud
Gloucestershire · GL5 2BU

First published 1995

Copyright © Robert Cook, 1995

Cover photographs: front: Bletchley station,
Easter Monday 1955; *back*: Bletchley Junction,
1928. *Title-page photograph*: Bletchley station,
1950s. (British Railways)

British Library Cataloguing in Publication Data.
A catalogue record for this book is available from
the British Library.

ISBN 0-7509-0901-3

Typeset in 9/10 Sabon.
Typesetting and origination by
Alan Sutton Publishing Limited.
Printed in Great Britain by
Hartnolls, Bodmin, Cornwall.

Bletchley Road, pictured from the Fenny Stratford (east) end. Pupils from Leon School, on the left, would soon be transferred to a larger purpose-built school by the Lakes estate. This was the early 1950s and a turning-point in Bletchley's history. London overspill was on the way.

Contents

Ken Barrow took this view, looking east towards Bletchley Road, from the railway bridge. The London Brick Company's AEC Mercury, passing the Park Hotel, dates the photograph to around 1958. The row of tin shops visible just past the railings on the left were very popular and included Mr Hurst's bicycle shop, Elizabeth's hat shop and the finest fish and chip shop in town.

Introduction

To the outsider or newcomer Bletchley and Fenny Stratford may seem as one place. They might even be judged no more than a suburb of Milton Keynes New Town. But each place has its own separate history and identity.

When the energetic George Temple Grenville, Marquess of Buckingham, backed the Grand Junction Canal in 1792 he put Fenny Stratford on the map. The canal reached there in 1800, bringing increased trade, prosperity and growth. Meanwhile, just over a mile to the south-west, Bletchley slumbered.

Named after the Saxon Blecca, who made a clearing (ley) in the woodland called Whaddon Chase, Bletchley for a long while remained a village. Walter Giffard was Lord of the Manor in 1092 and the title passed to Richard de Clare. Richard's daughter married John de Grey de Wilton and his name lives on through Wilton Hall, Wilton Avenue and the Lord Grey School. Conflicts with Henry VIII and later the Stuarts damaged the family's fortunes, and other great names came to prominence. Sir George Villiers, Earl of Buckingham, received the lands in 1623 and sold them to Charles III's doctor friend, Thomas Willis, in 1674. His grandson, Browne Willis, inherited the manor in 1699. Browne Willis repaired and decorated Bletchley Church and did much for Fenny Stratford, reviving its market and rebuilding the church after a fire in 1746. Given Fenny's position on the old Roman Watling Street, it is surprising that its centre did not dominate the region when the railways came in 1838.

By coincidence Browne Willis's wife was a direct descendant of Walter Giffard, who came to England with William the Conqueror in 1066. Two miles west of Bletchley, the large village of Newton Longville still bears his imprint. In the twelfth century Giffard founded a Benedictine priory at Longueville in Normandy, and established a cell to this priory in the place he named Newton Longueville.

All the old feudal ways came under threat in 1838 when the London Birmingham Railway Company arrived. But for the feudal landlords, such as the Temple family of Stowe, the company's chief engineer, Robert Stephenson, might have chosen a route through Buckingham. Bletchley was further from their homes, so was on a route less likely to provoke major opposition and obstruction.

So Bletchley was put on the map and was soon growing fast towards Fenny Stratford and Watling Street. Ideally situated for expansion in the Ouzel Valley, in the shadow of the beautiful Brickhills to the south-east, and with prime farmland all around, it offered the best of all worlds.

Beneath the surface ran a belt of carboniferous Oxford Clay, which was first discovered at Fletton, near Peterborough, in 1888. The Fletton brick revolution encouraged the London Brick Company (LBC) to move into the area in 1925. It was an excellent companion to the booming railway, sending train loads of bricks from its sidings to destinations all over the country. Other little companies such as Cooks and Beacon brushes also blossomed, though the region was still mainly agricultural.

In 1883 financier Sir Herbert Leon had bought Bletchley Park estate and the new mansion, built on the site of Browne Willis's Water Hall. Sir Herbert was a great benefactor but never a fan of the noisy trains that kept him company next door.

For a long time Bletchley remained fairly small and compact, and social differences were few and manageable. After the Second World War London could not cope with the housing demand, and there were dreams of giving city dwellers a better life in the countryside. Bricks were in high demand for postwar reconstruction and LBC's Bletchley works near Newton Longville was already attracting European workers as well as Londoners. Bletchley began to expand. A new estate along Whaddon Way opened a pub aptly named The Satellite – now interestingly renamed The Wishing Well.

When the South East Development Plan was published in the sixties, the town held its breath. Would Bletchley become just a suburb of a planned new city in north Buckinghamshire? There was already controversy that existing overspill policies had made Bletchley a dumping ground for London's problem families.

In 1965 Housing Minister Dick Crossman and Prime Minister Harold Wilson both attended public meetings at Wilton Hall to allay fears. Councillors flew to Sweden in March 1965 to study futuristic blocks of flats. There was talk of building similar ones next to a hospital being planned for land off Whalley Drive. Outspoken Council Chairman Jim Cassidy, a Scottish newcomer via London, said he would 'fight for the new city, for Bletchley'.

Bletchley is now part of that new city, Milton Keynes (still officially a town), but has its own designated area within it. The population had reached 37,395 at the 1991 census. There is evidence that many of these people are drawn towards Milton Keynes as the focus of their shopping and leisure activities. Though Bletchley still has its share of industry, such as the world-famous Marshall Amplification, many of its older elements have disappeared or been run down. The railway is a shadow of its former self and the brickworks has gone, following the Hanson takeover of the LBC. I hope that it is not symbolic of our age that the old brickworks' clay pits are now at the centre of a thriving refuse-disposal business. The pretty village of Newton Longville has exchanged a fleet of brick lorries for a multitude of dustcarts and container lorries. It might be said that it has seen fewer changes than most other parts of the Bletchley area. At the time of the city plan, Newton Longville was keen to stay outside Milton Keynes' boundaries. But with a trend toward relentless in-filling there is no telling what the future holds. The only growing certainty is in the values of the past.

Robert Cook
October 1995

The walls come tumbling down at Mount Pleasant, Fenny Stratford, early 1960s. A new city is planned for the area and Bletchley looks for a new identity within or without it.

Section One

STREET WISE

The plaque on Denbigh Bridge states that the
railway formerly ended at The Denbigh Arms.
There passengers travelling between London and
Birmingham reposed before a stage-coach took
them on to another section of railway at Rugby,
run by another company.

Brickhill crossroads near Fenny Stratford before the road was widened, c. 1897. The road surface shows signs of its annual dressing of gas tar topped with sand (see p. 17). The London–Holyhead telegraph poles stand proud as state-of-the-art communications hardware. At least the road is quiet. Donald Fraser Blane notes: 'When I was a boy the only car seen on the road was the chauffeur-driven Rolls-Royce carrying the Duke of Bedford from Woburn to catch the morning fast train to London.'

The still-rural character of this area was evident in 1949, when J.H. Peel wrote, in *Buckinghamshire Footpath*: 'A few yards beyond the Denbigh Arms is a sign-post pointing in the direction of Simpson [north], but any motorist who is deceived by it will find his machine in some discomfort, for the way is no more than a reinforced cart track; indeed when we were children, we christened it Blackberry Lane, from many expeditions there with our grandfather. I have an especial affection for this lane, since the best part of my childhood was spent at Staple Hall, not far away from it; a pleasant country house that once had its orchard and fruit garden and a fine sweep of lawn, but is today given over to builders.' Peel went on to lament that the only thing spoiling Blackberry Lane was gypsies camped along the furzy bank, grown so 'sluttish' that 'tin cans, burned-out kettles, newspapers, and the pink parts of feminine underwear are now to be found hanging from profuse blackberry bushes, or broadcast willy-nilly in dells and upon mole hills'.

Water Eaton village, south of Bletchley, at the turn of the century. A few of the old village features remain to distinguish this area from the rest of Bletchley.

There were still plenty of wide open spaces around Bletchley in 1920. This view of Three Trees Square shows Chandler's shop. From the front parlour, which had a bell over the door, Mrs Chandler served the vital goods, while her husband delivered the mail around what was still little more than a village.

Bletchley Road, looking towards Fenny Stratford, in Edwardian times. There were very few shops here at this time – the road remained largely residential until the 1920s. Locals walked or cycled to shops in Aylesbury Street, Fenny Stratford. The children in this picture could easily escape the town's confines, with the countryside so close. In springtime boys used to search for birds' eggs. They would make pin holes in the pretty shells and blow out the yolk, then take the eggs home to add to their collection.

Collecting birds' eggs is now illegal, but there are fewer hedgerows and trees for the birds to nest in, as fields have become larger and fewer. Nowadays farmers work by a different set of rules, producing more food on less land, but at some cost to nature.

Nash's toyshop, on the left, was an Aladdin's cave of toys. The houses, with their big bay windows, were ideal for conversion into shops as trade grew along the thoroughfare. Makeshift canopies were attached to increase the space for goods. Children could test their new whips and tops on the wide quiet road. If they could not afford a toy, they could always skate their hob-nailed boots along the pavement and make sparks fly for fun.

The Eight Bells Inn in Buckingham Road was probably named after the eight daughters of the Selby Lowndes, who lived at Elmers near the church. Edward, Prince of Wales, hunted with the Whaddon Chase during the 1920s because foot and mouth disease had closed down his regular hunting ground, the Quorn in Warwickshire. He used to meet with other huntsmen outside this pub on the green.

Bletchley Road in Edwardian times. Schoolchildren would walk along here carrying their white bread spread with margarine and blackberry jam and a piece of home-made cake for afters – all wrapped in newspaper. Donald Fraser Blane recalls that his mother made 100 lb of jam each season.

Compare this photograph with the one on p. 4. The Belisha beacons have been installed in line with recent legislation in this view of Buckingham Road by the Park Hotel (the point at which it merges with Bletchley Road), 1930s. The old tin shops on the left were demolished when the railway flyover was built in 1958–9. This little row served the neighbourhood well. It was a good place to buy two-wheeled transport. Opposite Mr Hurst's shop (note the motor bikes outside, in the left distance) was Baldry's bicycle shop. This business blossomed into a taxi and coach firm, starting with a pre-war Austin 10 car.

Looking along Bletchley Road towards Fenny Stratford, Leon School is on the right – the lady on the bicycle is possibly an escaping mistress! At least all is serene outside. All eight of Charlie Blane's children attended the school and the youngest, Martin, remembers that the headmaster was nearly as wide as he was tall. 'If anybody did anything wrong, they were sent along to see him. He'd ask what they'd done and then out would come the strap from his drawer. He said to each of us Blanes as we came along, that we weren't as good as the last.'

Victoria Road, Fenny Stratford, early 1920s. Cook's brush factory was on the right-hand side, just past the bend. Beacons and Jimmy Roots also made brushes, in Tavistock Street. It used to be said that Bletchley was all bricks, brushes and railways.

Swan Corner, High Street, Bletchley.

Though still recognizable as Fenny Stratford, this 1920s scene at Swan Corner has changed considerably. Durans the opticians, on the left, has made way for new flats and courtyards. More modern houses have replaced the old terraces behind the shop and the road is wider. The Swan Hotel remains but The Rose and Crown pub was demolished and the whole area is now dominated by a large roundabout and busy junction. Fenny Stratford has long since been absorbed by Bletchley, which itself is now part of Milton Keynes. Situated on the Roman Watling Street, Fenny Stratford acts as a gateway to the city from the south. It is all a far cry from its origins as an Iron Age settlement and later as the site of a Roman trading post at Magiovinium (near Bow Brickhill).

Aylesbury Street, Bletchley.

A fine view of Aylesbury Street, Fenny Stratford, late 1920s. Here the gas street lamps are still in place. Electricity, supplied from Northampton, did not arrive until 1930. Before that, coal gas produced at premises near The Navigation Inn, to the right of this picture, provided energy for streetlighting and domestic use. In the home it was obtained by putting pennies in a prepayment meter which was in a pantry under the stairs. The wide pavement in this picture was the site of the old livestock market.

Bridge Hotel, High Street (on Watling Street), looking towards the Brickhills. The large house on the left, just beyond the bridge, is now derelict and is a favourite site for flyposters. The old gasworks was built just behind this property. Coal came here by railway wagon – the Bletchley–Bedford line ran along the rear of the works – and was heated in the retort house. During this process gas escapes from the coal, and coke and tar are consequently formed. The tar was stored in tanks for use in road surfacing. The demise of the works came with the discovery of natural gas in the 1960s. Donald Fraser Blane had spent most of his working life at these works. He moved south when they closed and eventually to Canada, seeking further employment in the gas industry. This was rather adventurous for a man in his fifties but perhaps no different from the spirit that brought his father to Bletchley to work on the railway.

The Bridge Hotel in Fenny Stratford High Street looks very sedate in this 1920s picture. In the words of J.H. Peel: 'No man who knows Buckinghamshire will quarrel with me when I say that here is a county of repose and moderation; not flamboyant or startling.'

The canal bridge near The Navigation Inn, c. 1920. This photograph provides a better view of the large old house which loomed up in front of the gasworks. It looks like an ideal setting for a horror film but at the time was the office of the London County Insurance Company.

Fenny Stratford High Street, looking south, late 1890s. Polly Howard's shop is on the right, and giant telegraph poles are carrying hidden messages for an increasingly busy world. The telephone exchange (known then as a repeater station) is in the distance on the right.

Aylesbury Street, 1907. This was a vital shopping area but was still predominantly rural in character. Farm labourers numbered among the residents in these long-gone thatched cottages. Fast-food shops now thrive along this busy thoroughfare.

Hector Grace's lorry stands loaded with broken bricks from demolition. This was being carried out at Fernbank, Mount Pleasant, near the rear of Aylesbury Street on the Bletchley side. Hector started in business before the war as one of many private hauliers delivering bricks for the London Brick Company before it had its own fleet of lorries. He would not have treated the company's bricks so carelessly as he did these old ones. But nowadays no one would handle old bricks so badly, as they are more expensive than new ones. Building with old bricks gives the impression of a mature building and brings back some of the lost charm.

Fernbank was a row of ten terraced houses. Donald Fraser Blane lived on the other side of town, in similar accommodation at 14 Brooklands Road: 'It was in the middle of a terrace of about sixteen homes. There was a continuous blue brick pathway along the rear of the terrace. We had a small living-room kitchen which had a red and black tiled floor. The tiles were mostly covered with square-patterned linoleum. There was a sofa under which boots were stored at night. The kitchen table was covered with a light coloured oilcloth. There was a coal-fired range with an oven on one side and water boiler on the other, all recessed in an alcove. I do not remember the water boiler ever being used. It wasn't connected to anything and had a crack in it. A kettle . . . was our usual source of hot water. The coal range was cleaned every Saturday and polished with brushes [hence all the brush factories]. A coalman called each week with his horse and cart. Coal came in half hundredweight or hundredweight hessian sacks. He carried them on his back.'

Final days of Fernbank. It is a shame they demolished such a fine set of chimneys. Talking of chimneys, Donald Fraser Blane recalls: 'There was excitement in the street when the sweep was coming – everybody up early. We couldn't light the fire, so being winter we needed all our clothes on. The great moment for the children was when they went outside to see the brush come out of the top of the chimney pot.'

The washing is still out in one Fernbank backyard in spite of the dust – it wouldn't be long now. The view is from the private road which led to the back of The Three Tuns pub in the High Street. This alleyway also provided a short cut to the County cinema (known as the Palace) and the baker's shop.

Bletchley bus station viewed from the viaduct, July 1991. The bus park used to throng with proper double-deckers of the United Counties Fleet but deregulation brought the little German Hoppa Stoppa buses. These are seen here clustering by the equally modern structure of Stephenson House, next to the Brunel Centre – do these names really keep alive the glories of the bygone age of steam? At the closure of the Oxford–Cambridge line through Bletchley, Buckingham MP Robert Maxwell warned that 'bus operators can only operate on this line at the expense of providing an even worse service on routes in this area'. The alternative bus service soon withered along with many others, and I can remember waiting for hours on this windswept piece of tarmac for a Winslow bus that never came.

At least the fine view of the Brickhills on the horizon remains. The name Brickhills derives from the peculiar reddish hue of sandy soil outcropping there. The view of these hills was judged so fine that in the early 1950s the council charged its tenants an extra half crown a week to live in Pinewood Drive, which overlooked Brickhills. Stephenson House was built in the mid-1970s, cutting Buckingham/Bletchley Road off from the Queensway and necessitating a new loop road.

Section Two

LOSING STEAM

A presentation to Mrs Dora Prue at Bletchley station, 14 July 1955.

A view of the line and lever frame at Bletchley No. 1 signal-box (south end), 18 November 1956. These were the final days of steam on a line which had a glorious history, involving the London & North Western Railway (LNWR), London, Midland & Scottish (LMS) and Oxford–Cambridge 'Varsity Line'. Many famous engines had passed this way, but the railways were losing steam in more ways than one. There were moments when it seemed that the railways would get the serious investment they needed. For example, a new flyover was built to connect with a planned new goods yard at Swanbourne sidings. But as cross-country lines were closed, the network's goods potential dwindled and a mania for the dubious freedom offered by the motor car put new limits on the service. (Ken Barrow)

There were not many winters left for Bletchley steam when this snowy view of the station approach was captured on the morning of 19 January 1955. The station had already seen some changes by this time, notably the LNWR giving way to the LMS in 1923. This had meant that carriages had to be painted red instead of chocolate and white. Nationalization brought bigger changes, with investment in new forms of motive power and hopes for a great future. But ideas for real improvements got lost among political arguments and vested interests. (Ken Barrow)

Much has been written of Bletchley's railway past. This photograph shows Bletchley Junction in 1928. At that time a traveller informed *Punch* that the junction was 'standing queen-like in the valley of the Great Ouse' and that it 'has, in spite of neither being the seat of a university nor a cathedral town, an attractiveness of its own which causes many visitors to loiter spellbound in its precincts and some even to make a prolonged stay'. Sadly the elegant bustling atmosphere has gone. The station's frilled canopies no longer ring and echo to the whistle and whoosh of the 'Royal Scot', 'Coronation Scot' or 'Mid-Day Scot', headed by an impressive Stanier 'Pacific' locomotive. Anonymous expresses still thunder through and commuter trains stop but it seems so uniform and dull. Milton Keynes Central usurped the station's premier role in 1982.

The best that can be said is that there is a lot less labour and danger on the railway now. Platelayer Bob North was lucky to survive a serious accident along the Buckingham branch line in the late 1940s. Because of his injury he was transferred to flagging duties in the Bletchley area. 'I remember the old "Caledonian" express. We used to call it "the killer". I saw two men and a ganger working as it come along. I shouted but it were too late.'

Fred Bateman recalls the work being hard. 'But we were interested in our jobs and all mucked in. My first thirty-one years were with the LMS as a callboy, getting the drivers up out of bed, then as a cleaner, fireman, main-line driver and shift foreman. We had seventy locomotives on shed, half in steam [with the fires lit and the boilers producing steam; it took hours to get fires up to a sufficient heat, so half were kept going continually]. On a given signal from the selected timekeeper at midnight, the whistles and Stanier hooters were opened up for about ten minutes to welcome in the new year.' (Hunting Aero Films)

The approach to Bletchley station, with the Railway Hotel on the right, February 1950. (British Railways)

Many of the old traditions had already passed when this picture of the old station front was taken in May 1962. The façade itself would soon follow. (British Railways)

Bletchley post office, next to the station, 1940s. The Temperance Tea Rooms, on the right, indicate the fervour with which some groups waged war against the demon drink. Cyril Freeman spent a lot of his working life at the post office after the war, with about fifty others whom he described as a good bunch. 'I went there in 1947. They were a happy crowd. There were three shifts: the early town walk, early rural and late rural. I started on £4 a week. Inspector Blake was the boss and Wilson was the Post Master. On nights you had to meet the paper train. We sorted and despatched the mail. The bags were hung by the platform in leather pouches. The mail coaches had a net and scooped them off in a split second.

When the train robbery happened in 1963, someone must have been there at Glasgow where it started to tell them the mail coach was coupled to the engine. They faked a red signal at Cheddington Bridge and uncoupled it from the rest of the train, forcing the driver to take it to a siding. First thing I heard of it was next morning when I went to work and there were a lot of police about.'

That wasn't the only moment of drama. Cyril recalls an incident in the late 1960s: 'Inspector George Eames come rushing up saying "Quick, ring the police, there's a bomb." He had this parcel and it were ticking. Eventually we undid it in the parcel office. It was a toy train!' (British Railways)

A head-on collision at Bletchley station, 13 October 1939. Driver Irving Butler lay dead under the shunting engine for nineteen hours. Cyril Freeman was in the army and remembers hearing about it on the radio news. He knew his fiancée, Annie Budd, would have been arriving at the station at around the time of the crash, and it was a while before he knew she was safe. (British Railways)

Bletchley station refreshment room, 28 February 1950. It had been nicely refurbished after it was damaged in the 1939 crash. At this time there were still many service uniforms about, to look after a dying British Empire. Still, at least it was service with a genuine smile! (British Railways)

The wall between the locomotive depot and the spinney, November 1956. (Ken Barrow)

The old railwaymen knew a bit about animals. They kept horses to shunt loose wagons and pull delivery carts around town. So when anyone else's animals were carried by train, they did not expect them to go miles without refreshment. They would be offloaded, put into pens, fed and loaded on to a different train if the one they came in could not wait. Here Nobby Clarke is unloading pigs, March 1953. (Ken Barrow)

Bletchley goods yard, March 1953. These railway pig pens are full of animals ready to be loaded on to waiting goods wagons. (Ken Barrow)

The railway goods business was still going strong when this picture was taken in April 1963. Sadly it was not good enough to justify the flyover (in the background), which was then fairly new and linked Bletchley with the east–west Varsity Line. (B. Brooksbank)

Releasing pigeons on Bletchley station, Easter Monday 1955. The railway carried a lot of pigeons for the popular working men's sport of pigeon racing. British Railways offered a special service to pigeon fanciers: it could send the birds anywhere in the country. The baskets were usually carried in the guard's van and kept sealed until the moment of release. If staff members were lucky they might find a half crown stuck to the seal as a tip. A letter would be posted to the birds' owner telling the exact time of release. This practice provided an important training exercise for serious racers. (Ken Barrow)

A Diesel Multiple Unit train arrives from Cambridge via Bedford, 1964. These were the last days of the Varsity Line, which had opened in 1862 thanks to engineers such as Thomas Brassey and the incredible efforts of an army of navvies. It may have involved considerable travail to create the line but it took only the pen of one person, Labour Transport Minister Barbara Castle, to close it. This happened in 1967, in spite of Dr Beeching's recommendation that the line should stay open. Her decision seems remarkable considering that plans for the new city of Milton Keynes were being openly discussed in 1965. There seems to have been little thought towards creating a diversified transport system for such a massive development. Instead Mrs Castle appeared to be happy to accept British Railways' claims that the line was losing more than £100,000 a year under existing circumstances. The National Union of Railwaymen hotly disputed British Railways' figures in a report called 'The University Lines: The National Fraud'.

Before that the line had an illustrious history, connecting two world-famous centres of learning and prime agricultural market centres. Wartime created enormous activity, such as moving service personnel and weapons. Fred Bateman remembers driving petrol trains and bombs that 'looked like overgrown dustbins' with fins – the Americans nicknamed them 'Cookies'.

Less obvious was the passage of 'boffins' from London and the university towns to Bletchley Park and neighbouring intelligence bases. Baden Powell from Simpson village recalls that one of these was the writer Angus Wilson, who became Professor of English at the University of East Anglia: 'He had a little squeaky voice, was quite tiny, wore fancy-coloured socks and used to be the librarian at the British Museum. He couldn't do anything practical. He was billeted with my mother-in-law at Simpson.' (H.L. Holland)

A lonely water crane, winter 1966. All other evidence of Bletchley steam loco sheds has gone. The demolition contractor's machine stands next to a new electric loco. Donald Fraser Blane recalls: 'Friday was pay day. When my father was away working, one of the older boys would visit the loco shed to draw his pay. It was fascinating to be so close to the engines. The pay would be in a small cylinder which had a metal label with dad's number on it. We hurried home to mother for her to check it. The average pay was £2 to £3 a week in the 1920s for a fifty-hour week.' (Colin Stacey)

In 1966 British Railways' London Midland Region Chairman, H.C. Johnson, announced that Bletchley station would receive a facelift. This would include a new car-park for 336 cars on the site of the old steam-engine sheds. The picture shows the ground cleared ready for the tarmac. (Colin Stacey)

The redundant Bletchley water tower, which supplied water for steam-engine boilers, 1966. Underneath was a building where drivers and firemen could stay if they were away from home overnight. They would pick up another train next morning and return to their own loco depot. (Colin Stacey)

Experimental trains were not new to Bletchley when this picture was taken, on 5 April 1955. This one is London bound, hauled by locomotive No. 10201. (Ken Barrow)

These were the days, back in the fifties, when many little boys wanted to be engine drivers. The next best thing was to be a train spotter, like these two on Bletchley station. The big engines let you know which they were in those days, with their gleaming paintwork, nameplates and brass, all gone in a flash but the sound lingered in your ears. There was no need for pop stars!

The railway bridge over Buckingham Road, 1958. The Revd Thomas D. Broughton, Rector of Bletchley (1832–61), spent a day counting trains passing the level-crossing, as part of a campaign to get this bridge built. In front of the bridge the flyover is under construction. (British Railways)

Construction of the flyover is well under way, 1959. The Park Hotel is on the left and the carriage sheds are top right, just above the signal-box. In the left distance are the chimneys of the brickworks. (British Railways)

The flyover is ready, and a heavy goods train heads over it past the Newfoundout pond, towards Oxford, summer 1960. Martin Blane recalls his 1920s childhood: 'Ash from the steam-engine fire-boxes was dumped in the Newfoundout, making the water very mucky. We used to run along the brick dividers which cut it into sections. One day I slipped backwards. My mother said "A bath for you, my lad" when I got home, then she clipped my ear.' (Colin Stacey)

The flyover was still busy when this picture was taken of engine No. 75038, 7 July 1964. But there was still no sign of the marshalling yard at Swanbourne and never would be. Passenger services on the Oxford branch line were converted to diesel in November 1959. Over a period of two years, losses were reduced from £70,000 to £26,000 per annum. The branch service to Buckingham ceased in September 1964. (Colin Stacey)

The driver of this 'Black 5' locomotive would have gained a good view of the brickworks chimneys as he rattled past Whiteley Crescent on his way to Swanbourne sidings, late 1950s. The sidings closed in March 1967. (D. Barrow)

Martin Blane remembers travelling through this tunnel in the late 1950s on his way to Cheddington to take the Aylesbury branch. 'Working for the Co-op Insurance Company, I used to visit the Aylesbury office regularly. On this particular occasion we were approaching the tunnel and I was in a compartment with an elderly gent. He seemed to be taken ill. I said, "Are you all right, old chap?" then realized he had died. It didn't worry me. I always accepted that death was something that happens to us all.'

Baden Powell was in a reserved occupation during the Second World War. Working for the Northampton Electric Light Company, he was responsible for wiring maintenance at Bletchley Park. At other times he served with the Home Guard, and remembers guarding this signal-box at Denbigh Bridge (pictured here in 1954) with a First World War rifle. (Colin Stacey)

The same bridge in December 1982. Electrification has arrived and a large power-box at Bletchley has removed the need for the signal-box. During the war, with all the train movements, signal personnel were vital. Bletchley engine driver Fred Bateman would not have met his young Welsh wife, Ethel Roberts, if the essential works order had not diverted her from Bletchley Park to become a signalwoman. (Colin Stacey)

The Bletchley–Cambridge branch line, photographed by a signalman Jack Bromfield, late 1940s. The LNWR-type signal-box is still there. In 1930 a wreath-bedecked train had passed by this spot, carrying the coffins of the R101 crash victims. The train was on its way to Cardington, where the R101 had been built.

Fenny Stratford level-crossing, Simpson Road, late 1940s. This is still in use, as plans to close the Bletchley–Bedford section of the old Varsity Line have been resisted since 1972. The station was built with fancy Gothic brick chimneys and half-timbering, because the Duke of Bedford wanted it to blend with his estate. The signal-box has since been resited.

Bletchley station, 1964. Syd Final looks very impressive in his gold-braided cap, as he looks down to have a word with Les Pitt on the track. (Colin Stacey)

This chirpy-looking fellow is Ken Barrow. He is working in the station booking-office following the station improvements in 1952. Ken was a keen and skilled amateur photographer. (Ken Barrow)

The station worked round the clock and there was a large staff. Here is Ken Barrow's colleague, Fred Robinson, March 1957. (Ken Barrow)

Ken strikes again! Here is a beautiful shot of a relaxed 'Dink' Thurlow in Bletchley goods account office, March 1954. (Ken Barrow)

Denis Comerford receives a watch and handshake from a British Railways manager at Bletchley Railwaymen's Club, 1968. Denis, like so many, followed in his father's footsteps. One of his earliest jobs was inspecting Stephenson's masterpiece, Claycross Tunnel, in the 1920s: 'We checked it just with headlamps. Dark, damp and coated with soot it was, and smelling of old steam engines.'

Denis moved down to work as a relief signalman on the Oxford–Cambridge line in 1937. He remembers fellow signalman Harold McLernon: 'He was an ex-sergeant, Royal Corps of Signals, and brought his army training with him. He was always there five minutes before start of shift and thrived on rules and regulations.'

Denis was made redundant when the branch line closed. He received a £415 lump sum and weekly payments of £4 8s 8d for two weeks, twenty-six weeks at 11s 8d and twenty-two weeks at £4 8s 8d should he remain unemployed. British Railways probably employed a lot of expensive staff to work out redundancy formulas like that!

The post office at Bletchley station, just before demolition, June 1982. A piece of history would soon be gone. Those were the days when Cyril Freeman drove his van out on the early rural run to Simpson and locals cooked him breakfast in their cottages. (Colin Stacey)

The post office was far too small for modern needs. Here the sorting-office roof comes tumbling down, soon to be followed by the rest of the old edifice. Bletchley was now part of Milton Keynes New Town and large modern computerized facilities had been established. (Colin Stacey)

The Metro-Cammell 'Blue Pullman' passes through Bletchley with a football special, 1963. This type of train was introduced in May 1959 and was the forerunner of the modern Intercity train. (Colin Stacey)

The ill-fated tilting Advanced Passenger Train (APT), which was tested on the Euston main line, is seen here halted at Sixty Steps, Bletchley, early 1980s. (Colin Stacey)

Bletchley power-box, looking south-east, early 1980s. This facility opened in June 1965. The signalman's job was thereafter much gentler toil. (Colin Stacey)

Stephenson House looms up over the rim of the flyover, July 1991. It is viewed from a Bedford-bound special train which has run up from Oxford as part of the Oxford Bucks Rail Action Campaign (OBRAC). The aim of the campaign was to re-open the line to regular passenger services. The line had cost £20,300 a mile to build in 1851, and surpassed the £10,000 a year it was expected to earn. When it closed, Robert Maxwell MP commented: 'I have been convinced all along that the Ministry of Transport have made a ghastly mistake.'

FORTUNE

Horace Rowe at the controls of the Bletchley
brickworks 'navvy' which he helped to assemble in
1930 and drove until his retirement in 1980.

An aerial view of Bletchley town centre, 1928. As can be seen, there was plenty of countryside for children to roam in, allotments to cultivate and fields where farmers could grow organic food. Martin Blane recalls that the field near where the leisure centre was built once had a market with gas-lit stalls in the winter: 'They used tilly lamps, as we called them. This same field, next to The New Inn, was where they held big funfairs and circuses. It was the highlight of the town. We liked Angel Dindol's shop too. It had an angel statue in a niche out front. Dindol was a Jew. He sold clothes. That was well before the war. Bletchley had some interesting sights in the old days.'

Oliver Wells JP was Secretary of Bletchley Co-op's Educational Committee, formed in 1896. He lost both legs in an accident while working on the railway. He overcame his handicap to ride a motor cycle with sidecar in the 1930s. Although Bletchley was surrounded by pastures of Conservatives, railway traditions fostered Socialism. Oliver was active in Labour politics and was a prominent councillor.

Mrs L. Caldwell was Secretary of the Bletchley branch of the Women's Co-operative Guild in 1934. The local Co-op movement was started by railway workers in 1884, buying essential goods in bulk and selling cheap to members. The Women's Guild encouraged teaching and discussions to promote the principles of cooperation and so increase trade and membership of the movement.

Jack Goodwin, President of the Bletchley & District Co-operative Society, pictured during the society's golden jubilee year, 1934. The society's first meeting was held at Bletchley station on 10 December 1883 (although the society didn't start officially until 1884). The society aimed to raise capital by selling two hundred shares at 10s each. A Mr Simmonds was elected president but he had a fatal accident in the railway yard immediately after the meeting and was replaced by Mr Piper at the second meeting, on 31 December.

The pioneers opened an account in Bassetts Bank in Park Street and approached the owner of this shop for a tenancy. This first shop was opened in February 1884 and Mr Bailey, from Chipping Norton, became manager. The town crier advertised the business around Fenny Stratford and Bletchley, and the seal of the society became a railway engine named *Unity*.

At the start the society made food deliveries by handcart. To get bread to outlying areas it rented a bakery in Winslow in 1922. But after five years baking was centralized in Bletchley and motor vans took over deliveries to rural areas. In 1919 the society opened a butchery and slaughterhouse in Bletchley. It handled 165 tons of meat annually, valued at £15,000 by the mid-1930s.

The Co-op's original premises were destroyed by an arsonist, who happened to be an insurance agent! This fine Co-op drapery store opened in Bletchley Road in October 1927.

Part of the Co-op's delivery fleet near the football ground, 1927. Baden Powell remembers the benefit of delivery men carrying messages for the old folk. Roly Doggett recalls the pleasures, during the school holidays, of travelling in his father Arthur's Co-op baker's van through country lanes to far-flung outposts such as Tingewick. Even I remember, as a boy, waiting for the van to bring us apple turnovers and doughnuts, in the final days of the business.

The Co-op's Jubilee Building, Bletchley Road, opened in 1934 and up until the 1960s was a symbol of the society's excellence (a large department store now occupies this site). As part of the 1934 jubilee celebrations the Co-op Educational Committee arranged a fourteen-day outdoor campaign throughout the society's large rural catchment area. Fred Longden, a former MP (Co-operative), was engaged as lecturer, and he addressed thirty meetings, assisted by a loudspeaker van.

Sheep pens at Fenny Stratford market, Aylesbury Street. Cattle were sold in a yard accessible via the gap in the buildings. The shop to the left of the gap was Moss's grocer's, where Bob Blane was sent in the 1920s for a Bath chap. He thought his workmates were playing a trick, but was handed half a smoked pig's head. The market sold most edible farm animals.

Fenny Stratford enjoyed brief prosperity when the Grand Junction Canal was built, between 1792 and 1800. This view shows a barge leaving the wharf after unloading maize for the brewing process at the premises of Valentine, Ord and Nagel, on the left. The Bridge Hotel, Watling Street, stands to the left of the bridge.

The Red Lion Inn and locks at Fenny Stratford, early this century. The wharf for the Rowlands timber yard was close by. Mr Hillard used to collect trees for the sawmill and carry them on a wagon hauled by a team of four or six horses.

Wagon drivers and boys in knickerbockers pose outside The Navigation Inn, just beyond the turning to the Fenny Stratford locks. Canalside inns had their heyday until the railway arrived. Then in 1846, through the patronage of the Duke of Bedford, a branch line was completed, linking Fenny Stratford and Bedford. Thus Fenny's prosperity was revived.

A boat passes Water Eaton Mill on the Grand Junction Canal (later known as Grand Union), 1950s. The area has not changed significantly, but there are signs that more development is in the offing. The canal is still busy, but the traffic is now mainly pleasure boats. Pubs such as The Bridge Hotel and Red Lion Inn have therefore enjoyed a revival of fortunes, along with the nostalgia market.

Vaughan, the newsagent's and general shop, Watling Street, 1920s. Note the fine old cigarette machine attached to the wall inside the doorway. Smoking was considered beneficial in those days.

Polly Howard and her son kept this shop in Fenny High Street until she retired in 1928. Mrs Sarah Howard, pictured in the doorway, ran it for the next five years. Above her, the advertisement for Zebra black lead grate polish says it all about a bygone age. Inside were three sets of scales: one for butter, cheese, lard, bacon and other groceries, another for thick twists of tobacco, and another for the children's suckers, acid drops, etc. The shelves were crammed with all that the local folk might need, from gas mantles to skipping-ropes and dolls. The shop closed in 1958 and was demolished when Watling Street (the A5) was widened at Church Corner. Behind the shop a cluster of tiny houses (Mount Pleasant) was also demolished.

Edgar Hill's shop in Bletchley Road, 1920s. Mr Hill was a debonair provider of footwear. Martin Blane recalls: 'At school, boys wore heavy boots with studs [hobnails]. At the weekend father inspected to see how many studs had gone due to us skating on them along the pavement.'

NEAL'S STORES

The Toy and Pram People

Bletchley Rd., Bletchley, Bucks

Telephone: Bletchley 2822

'SEVERES' by *Wilson*

28 gns.

● FREE DELIVERY

Bletchley was a growing town in the early 1950s and mothers needed prams. Neal's Stores, on the corner of Oxford Street, was there to provide the best, and all the toys a growing child might need. This shop replaced Bollen's sweets and cigarette store. Jack Blane remembers being sent to Bollen's by his older brothers for a tin of elbow grease, in the 1920s. Mr Bollen said, 'Sorry, we don't stock it!' Neal's moved to Milton Keynes city centre in the early 1980s but has now closed down.

Prams congest the pavement outside Bletchley Road post office, 1959. This section of Bletchley Road is now renamed Queensway. The population of the town was 10,000 in 1952, before the Town Development Act led the Urban District Council to take London overspill. Grants were given to build housing and improve facilities, offering hope of greater trade and prosperity. New homes were built on the south-east side, near worked-out and water-filled brick-clay pits, and christened the Lakes estate. Though it lay in green surroundings, the estate was system built and high density, and soon became infamous for its social problems. Londoners, divorced from their traditional family roots, did not always feel at home here.

New families grew and prams and pushchairs were a common sight on the wide Queensway pavements. The shopping centre had to meet new needs, but in 1965 Bletchley Chamber of Trade's President, H.C. Weatherhead, said that the Council was trying to expand too quickly: 'This town has already suffered from premature development of Bletchley Road to a position well in advance of its population level and, if it is to be limited to a final population of 40,000, very little further development can be sustained if our friends in Aylesbury Street are to get a certain measure of help.'

Queensway, early 1970s. Prospective Conservative parliamentary candidate Elaine Kellett warned, while Milton Keynes was being planned, that Bletchley could prosper only as the centre of the new city or if it were far enough away to develop independently. Nothing could be worse than being on the edge. It would sap the life from Bletchley. The centre is still bustling here, but for how long?

Jim Marshall is one of the area's most dynamic entrepreneurs. Famous for his amplifiers throughout the world, his other enterprises included this lighting shop in Queensway. Joe Brown was sporting these late sixties/early seventies fashions when he came to open the premises, and here he poses with the staff. Joe was working as a steam-loco fireman when he came to fame in the early 1960s. Visiting Bletchley, town of trains, must have been quite nostalgic for him.

The famous Marshall signature over Jim's music shop at the top of Queensway. I remember going in there in 1981 to buy a tin whistle to amuse myself while I waited for customers at my market stall a few yards away. In this picture Jim Marshall poses with driver, Peter Aylemore, just before the Tour of Britain, July 1976.

The Bull Commercial Family Hotel and attached garage, Fenny Stratford, 1930s. The wall on the right belongs to St Martin's Church.

This may look like a Swiss ski-lift, but actually it is the ropeway which carried clay from the pits (Knot Holes) to the London Brick Company's press sheds in the 1930s. These works were started by Tommy Read, who made bricks by hand from the more plastic clay nearer the surface. A brick-making revolution had started 42 miles away at Fletton, near Peterborough, in 1888. The sale advertisement for the Fletton estate highlighted the presence of good brick clay near the surface, but few people anticipated that Hempsted Brothers would dig down as far as 90 ft to the lower Oxford Clay. This clay has a high carbon content, which meant that although a little coal dust (smudge) had to be added occasionally to keep the temperature up, no fuel was needed to bake the bricks once the first kiln full of bricks was burning. Waste heat was driven through flues to dry out the bricks in a neighbouring chamber. When the first lot of bricks was baked, the fire would then pass through and the dried bricks would ignite easily. The fire went round and round the rows of chambers, and the kilns never went out (except while they were used to store ammunition during the Second World War). Exhaust gases from the burning bricks went up the lines of tall chimneys.

J.C. Hill emerged as one of the most successful Fletton brickmakers and formed the first London Brick Company. The bricks were cheap and in demand. They were transported to growing towns and cities, including London. Through a series of mergers, necessary to cope with the interwar depression, the Stewart family became the driving force of the new London Brick Company, and it took over Read's in 1925.

Above: the London Brick Company inevitably dominated the cheap Fletton brick market. The Stewarts were great innovators and organizers, and they introduced the first mechanical device for digging clay: a shale planer imported from the USA. Previously, the clay had been dug by hand on terraces (benches) and dropped into railway wagons, with obvious dangers. This Ruston Bucyrus 135 was bought in 1929 and is pictured just before retirement in 1980. Affectionately called the 'old navvy', it stood at the base of the pit and dug upwards.

Left: the London Brick Company's Bletchley works manager, George Forbes, with Lady Stewart, who is receiving a bouquet at a works sports day, early 1950s. Her husband, Sir Malcolm, was chairman of what was very much a family business.

This overturned dumper replaced Jenny Widget's horse and cart in 1936 and was used to take brickbats (broken bricks) from the lorry-loading docks (Jenny Widget worked at the yard, collecting the brickbats). Here Foreman Mechanic Frank Oliver does his bosses' bidding, turning to hiss 'Eh, you can't take pictures here!'

Brickbats were not wasted, but crushed to make hardcore for internal roads or sold to builders. Driver Tom Bates was employed here from 1964 to 1974, when bricks were still loaded individually. He recalls: 'I came from London and was allocated a new house in Bletchley. Whilst delivering on a site, I would sling brickbats back on the lorry for use as hardcore for a garden path I was making back home. On one occasion I was doing this when an Irish labourer said, "Why are you doing that, driver?" Jokingly, I said, "I'm taking them back to the yard to be mended" and he replied, "Oh Jesus, we got thousands of them here," and proceeded to throw them on to my lorry.'

'Mashe' Walduck using his Hyster forklift truck to load a private contractor's lorry at Bletchley brickworks, mid-1950s. The weight of the load is making a visible impression on the vehicle's tyres. Before these US machines the loaders used handcarts.

Bricks pressed from the hard lower Oxford Clay were called 'greens' before they went into the Hoffman kilns, as pictured here in the mid-1960s. The kilns had a series of chambers, which held about 35,000 bricks each. When full, the chamber was closed up, using bricks laid without cement, and sealed with a clay mix called pug. The walls thus made were called wickets. Each one used between 1,500 and 1,850 bricks, and good wicket erectors such as Ken Rendall, pictured here, could set four chambers in a day. Eddy Dickens is barrowing the bricks.

Stan Hughes stands in front of a British Road Services lorry, early 1950s. At this time a nationalized haulage network had been imposed by the Labour Government to improve efficiency and coordinate road and rail transports. The returning Tories were soon to dispose of most of this network, much to the disapproval of Stan Hughes, I suspect. He was Branch Secretary of the Transport and General Workers Union. He also helped to build No. 1 brick press shed, before Tommy Read sold out to the London Brick Company. His son Albert remembers his father having some funny old sayings, such as 'my gonder' which meant 'bloody hell'. He would never swear because he was the local Methodist preacher. The Church was very important to him, as was the Parish Council. He also campaigned for Robert Maxwell MP. Not surprisingly, his nickname was 'Emp' (short for Emperor).

Bletchley works manager Ted Hersee (left), a former chief engineer from the main yard at Stewartby, presents a gift to Stan Parrott on his retirement. Stan began at Bletchley drawing baked bricks from kilns and finished up as ticket clerk at the company's smaller Jubilee works. This was connected to the main site by an internal track, known affectionately by returning ex-servicemen as the 'Burma Road'.

Maurice Dell demonstrating an unusual talent, 1950s. Maurice was one of the private hauliers who collected and delivered bricks from Bletchley brickworks. His brother-in-law, Reg Knapp, worked in the delivery ticket office and remembers how hauliers used to compete to be first through the Newton Road gates on a Saturday morning. Reg's career at the works had started in the 1930s, after a Merchant Navy shipmate suggested he should apply for a job there. Reg recalls surprising the locals by coming for the interview dressed in plus fours.

Wally Brown, just before his retirement from the brickworks stores, 1970s. He was reckoned to be a good lead hand at bowls. The works had a fine sporting tradition, which owed much to the efforts of Jim White. He had worked hard to establish a sports club and was a fine county bowls player.

Driver Jack Bromfield, home from serving with the RAF during the war, leans nonchalantly against the cab of his AEC Mammoth Major 8 brick lorry at the White Hut Café. The café stood on the old Brighton road and provided overnight accommodation for these trunk-route drivers. Jack enjoyed the freedom of the road but the job had its risks. 'There was no power steering and as far as the brakes were concerned, you sent a postcard to where you wanted to stop.'

Driver Sid Corby stands proudly on the back of his AEC Mercury brick lorry, 1958. This state-of-the-art vehicle is parked in Newton Road, not far from the yard. Drivers were expected to keep their vehicles clean, inside and out.

A new kiln and chimney nears completion at Bletchley brickworks, 1964. It was needed to meet a massive demand for bricks as the country prepared for more urbanization. Within twenty-five years that urbanization was to spread outwards from Milton Keynes, ready to engulf the brickworks. The site is now redundant following the Hanson takeover of the London Brick Company.

This fine view of the brickworks was taken by Reg Knapp on completion of the last chimney, 1964. The works garage is in the foreground, and loaded lorries are making their way up towards the press sheds and then through the main gate, on to the Newton Longville road. The first company lorries left the yard in 1937, on detachment from the Stewartby works. For years the London Brick Company called the bricks Phorpres, because they were pressed four times. The presses were powerful and serious injuries occurred before guards were put on to the machines.

Working on the kilns also had its hazards. The pace of loading and emptying the chambers was hectic and the heat remained intense even when the fire had moved on to the next lot of bricks to be baked. One of the hard men, and legends of the yard, was Jimmy Digdeeper, believed to be an Antipodean. He slept in the empty kilns, and there were fears that he might get baked with the bricks. Bert Viccars recalls that Jimmy took the bus to town one night and drank so heavily that he ate soap and went to wash in a brook in the yard, using the cheese he had bought for lunch!

Ruth Watson, far right, and her office colleagues, 1960s. As the company expanded, the brickworks needed more administration staff. It was all a far cry from the little shed at the end of the railway siding where Reg Knapp started working. Once the shed was nearly demolished by a runaway train, and the hole left in the wall made the morning's work very cold. Ruth Watson was Brickworks Jubilee Queen in September 1950 and married driver, and later foreman burner, Jack Bromfield.

Bletchley brickworks was very busy after the war, with so much rebuilding to be done. Workers were in short supply and for a while German prisoners-of-war filled the breach. The company recruited displaced European Voluntary Workers such as 'Johnny Piecework', pictured here receiving a retirement gift from manager Richard Blake in 1974.

Midge Day and steeplejacks at the top of the new brickworks chimney just after completion, 1964. The new kiln was necessary to meet a still-booming demand for bricks, at a time when Milton Keynes was not the only new town in the offing and estates were going up all over the Home Counties. Ray Akins recalled that steeplejacks sang louder the higher they built because they got paid more. Midge Day was way beyond the call of duty serving tea right up here!

Midge Day's father, Sidney Clark. He was a farmer and milkman at Newton Longville, and customers took their milk in jugs. Midge recalls wearing a navy gymslip at Bletchley School and never daring to argue with the teacher. She left school to work at Peak's clothing factory in Denbigh Road, making military coats and uniforms for the war effort.

A McCormick reaper at work on a north Bucks farm, early 1900s. It was being used to advertise Bletchley's Vulcan engineering works, which was an agent for McCormick. Agricultural engineers and seed specialists were a vital part of the local economy.

GROWN WITH
HADFIELD'S SPECIAL
CORN MANURE.
FOR AUTUMN DRESSING.

Hadfield's special corn manure was another vital aid to the harvest. This advertisement shows a rural scene near Fenny Stratford. When Milton Keynes New Town was mooted, farmers were outraged that any of this beautiful and productive countryside could be considered for urbanization and that it would bring an end to their way of life, when there was so much derelict inner-city land available.

Alf Baldry rides his customized penny farthing past his shop at the top of Bletchley Road, 1950s. Baldry's, next to Barclays Bank, was a successful local business. Cycling was a very popular sport and means of relaxation between the wars. Serious cyclists such as the Goodman brothers went further afield, to race with the Luton Wheelers, and achieved a fair degree of fame. Both brothers worked for the local Co-operative Society and had to fit in training after a hard day's work. Sadly both were killed on training expeditions. The increase in road traffic was making this simple form of transport less pleasant.

Cyclists and pedestrians contrast with the couple gliding past in the Jaguar XK120, on the old station approach road, Fenny Stratford. Railway Terrace, known as Company's Row, stands neatly on the horizon. At the turn of the century Charles Henry Blane came from Cambridgeshire to live at No. 9, and he worked in Bletchley as a locomotive fireman. This picture was taken a few years before the flyover and redevelopment came. Hands Garage, with a taxi parked in front, is on the right, next to stabling where some of the shunting horses were kept. Everything disappeared with redevelopment. A new approach road, Sherwood Way, was built. Then came a new fire station and police station, rendering facilities in Church Street and Simpson Road obsolete. (Ken Barrow)

A shop redevelopment site in Fenny Stratford, 1950s. Bletchley had been earmarked as a redevelopment area in Professor Abercrombie's Greater London Plan of 1944. The decision in 1967 not to make Bletchley the centre of that town raised traders' fears that their centre would go into decline.

Stephenson House, on the south side of the bus station, was a glittering step towards making Bletchley an attractive part of the Milton Keynes conurbation. On the north side, this old United Counties bus garage, described as the town's worst eyesore, had to go. In January 1992 'Better Bletchley' campaigner Vanessa Pyke said she was delighted. But two years later Albert Del Grosso, who lived nearby, was horrified to hear of a plan to replace the garage with a pub and restaurant.

There was some anger and opposition to the Urban District Council's plan to let Rodwell, London and Provincial Properties take responsibility for redeveloping the town. Traders feared that shops would outgrow demand. A desperate rush ensued to make Bletchley a viable alternative to the planned city centre of Milton Keynes, and one outcome was the resiting of the open market from one end of Queensway to the other. The new site was close to where the Halfway House pub had stood and was more accessible to Fenny Stratford residents. The new market had the benefit of a covered roof, but it was a dubious shelter. When I was trading there in 1981 the wind used to whistle along Queensway as if down a tunnel. I didn't even have the comfort of making much money from my secondhand-book stall.

The market superintendent, a large and scowling fellow, would never let me set up shop until a rival bookseller was well under way. Consequently, I missed the early trade of shop girls looking for a good Mills and Boon! My only comfort was the man selling baby clothes on the stall next to me. He had been made redundant from a local factory, but with so many babies being born, he was now on to a good thing. He used to encourage me with the words, 'You've got to keep going. We could all be in the Bahamas this time next year.' I never knew his name, I just called him the 'baby clothes man'. The market superintendent I called the 'Fat Controller', because he was so rude to me. One day in particular I recall, business was so slack that I put an armchair in the back of my big old Post Office van. I arranged it behind the stall, and with little expectation of custom sat down to read one of my assorted railway histories. My mind was somewhere along the Great Western Railway when a voice boomed out behind me: 'Oy! This is a market, not a place for reposing.'

These futuristic canopies, I am sad to say, were burned down by a vandal shortly after this picture was taken in the late 1980s. I don't know whether the BMW driving past is the baby clothes man, showing off his success around town, or whether he is in the Bahamas!

There is no doubt about the success of Jim Marshall, seen here receiving a Queen's Award for Industry from the Lord Lieutenant of Bucks, Sir John Freemantle, 1992. Milton Keynes Mayor, Les Hostler, is on the left and Barry Legg MP is on the right.

Jim Marshall's first association with music was as a singer and drummer in London before the war. Wartime experience in engineering developed his interest and aptitude for technology, and this eventually blended with his music interests. His first major success was a drum school in Southall, which nurtured some famous names, including Mitch Mitchell of the Jimmy Hendrix Experience. When Jim opened a music shop in 1960 he had no shortage of customers, thanks to the fact that his very satisfied pupils and their friends put the word around. Demand for better amplifiers led Jim to design and build his own in a garage behind the shop.

Bletchley seemed an ideal location for his expanding business. In May 1966 Marshall's moved into a 3,000 sq. ft factory in Lyon Road, and production increased 110 per cent over twelve months. Jim recognizes the value of a happy workforce and a small and dedicated management team. Now in Denbigh Road, the company has just completed a £5 million expansion, incorporating the latest technology. Jim says: 'You have to move with new ideas. You can't stand still.' Interestingly, his renowned and popular products include valve amplifiers.

Section Four

DELIGHTFUL WAYS

A group of local musicians at Freeman Memorial

Hall, Victoria Road, early 1900s.

Bletchley Sunday School treat at Great Linford, before the First World War. There were only simple pleasures to be enjoyed by the majority in those strict and work-filled times. This trip looks very disciplined but I am told there was one such outing to Stoke Hammond when the lucky people travelled by barge from Fenny Stratford. On arrival at a canalside inn the bargee got so drunk he fell into the water, much to the amusement of the children. Other exciting destinations included Bow Brickhill Woods and Wickstead Park, where there were lots of free amusements.

The Old Swan, Shenley Road. Mr Crane stands on the steps while some of his regulars gain support from the walls. Another prepares for a ride home across the winter landscape. The pub was open around the clock during Bletchley Feast and used to throng with noisy fairground folk. It was demolished in the 1890s.

The Shoulder of Mutton at the junction of Bletchley Road and Newton Road, 1930s. The edge of the brick-built extension is just visible on the right. The pub's clientele was expanding with the town. In 1944 magistrate Sir Everard Duncombe, concerned about the problems of enforcing licensing laws, was quoted in *Bletchley Gazette*: 'I know that the appearance of women of all ages is deceptive. It is difficult sometimes to know whether a girl is under eighteen. . . . It is a question of dress and additional decoration which helps the deception.'

The Shoulder of Mutton pub, which stood in an area called Three Trees Square, 1950s. The brick extension destroyed the old inn's beauty, and now all has gone. Some still remember playing games of marbles, hopscotch, hoops and spinning tops around the quiet green. The magistrate's report of 1944 spoke of action against five persons for drunkenness and stated that pubs had been well conducted; no actions were taken against licence holders. Those were the days!

The Plough, Water Eaton, 1930s. Charlie Fairey was the landlord and his brother Tom had a general store. The pub was demolished for road improvements but Richardson's farmhouse still stands opposite and is a home for battered wives. The white telephone-box was an interesting feature and stood near a duckpond.

Bletchley armistice celebrations, 1918.

Children of Bletchley Road School (formerly Leon School) performing the Spanish comic opera *The Bandolero*, February 1934. Lady Fanny Leon attended one performance and around a hundred children participated. The show raised a remarkable £128, which was spent on projection equipment.

Mr Muckley's Railway Choir, 1920s. In spite of its name it consisted entirely of schoolchildren. Children were so different then. Donald Fraser Blane, born on 19 October 1908, recalls: 'On Mondays we were usually allowed to sit at our classroom desks to eat our meal and then went out into the playground until the bell sounded. Typical dress for boys would be long black woollen stockings secured with black garters above the knee, a grey flannel shirt and jacket. Always lace-up boots when young, and perhaps a pair of shoes on Sunday after twelve years of age. The boots had to be polished with "blacking", which was solid in a tin and required some spit to soften it. Boys occasionally wore a cap. In summer they wore shorts and sometimes plimsolls. Girls wore black wool stockings with garters above the knee and a dress at least down to the calf of the leg. When they were twelve they might have a blouse and skirt. At home they wore a pinafore to protect their dress. On Sundays a boy wore a suit, if he had one, for Sunday School. His collar would be white celluloid, attached to the shirt with studs. Girls wore their best dresses.'

Brass bands were popular at village events. Here, band leader Mr Thomas poses at Sir Herbert Leon's Bletchley Park show, early 1930s.

And of course Mr Thomas brought his Bletchley Station Brass Band with him to delight the annual Bletchley Park show gathering!

A large advertisement for Sunlight soap, discovered on a wall of the old Co-op in Albert Street, suggested that the building might be the site of the old public baths. Tom Pacey remembered bathing in premises behind a cooked-meat shop in Bletchley Road in the 1920s. That was about the time when these young men were pictured enjoying the open-air pool on the Ouzel at Manor Fields, where they used a tin hut for changing rooms. Standing second from the left is Donald Fraser Blane. Bob Blane, standing on the right, became Co-op district manager during the halcyon days. The eight Blane brothers were known as the 'bullocks', because their curly fringes resembled those on Hereford cattle!

The County cinema, or Palace, Watling Street, Fenny Stratford, c. 1918. Roy Stockham recalls how films tended to break down. Martin Blane remembers paying a few pennies for Saturday Westerns and kids throwing orange peel at the screen. The County was one of the first fifty provincial cinemas to be built in 1911. It was very busy in wartime, showing epics such as *Sherlock Holmes' Secret Weapon* with Basil Rathbone. Its many proprietors included Amos Stephenson of the Fenny Stratford Gas Company, who sold it to Odeon in 1941. Odeon showed its last film, *Doctor at Large*, in June 1957.

The forced landing of Claude Grahame-White at Mount Farm, Simpson. He was participating in the London–Manchester Air Race, a new-found pleasure for the affluent classes. As the plane came down and ran along the ground it flipped on to its back. The following year, fog forced the first British commercial flight – carrying a load of boots – to land near Fenny Stratford.

Mr and Mrs Hurst, two of the new motoring generation, parked outside 52 Leon Avenue, early 1920s. Bletchley immigrant Herbert Ackroyd Stuart ought to be better known for his contribution to motoring. At his tiny Bletchley ironworks in Denmark Street, it is said some hot slag fell on oil in the foundry pit and exploded. This inspired his design of an oil engine, which was more like modern diesels than Dr Rudolf Diesel's original work. Imagine, if history had been different, drivers might be filling up with Ackroyd!

Bletchley Football Club, 1930. The team used to play on Market Field, which is now occupied by Sainsbury's store and car-park.

Bletchley LMS Football Club, 1947. This title was soon to be an anachronism, with railway nationalization imminent.

OUR HOUSE

This field behind the Park Hotel was the main sports ground until the cattle market took over in 1924. Shown here is one of the last football matches played on it.

Lady Leon provided an alternative ground for the Bletchley town cricket team at Bletchley Park, 1928. E.C. 'Barrel' Cook, seated third from the left, was captain.

T. Brace (centre) and H. Clarke (right) at a traditional ox roast. Events of this kind were organized as part of a major celebration, and this was probably for the silver jubilee of George V, in 1935.

Central Gardens, Bletchley, early 1950s. This was before the leisure centre came to dominate the area. These gardens were strictly for relaxation, but there were others for the more energetic. Martin Blane recalls: 'Good Friday was garden day. We used to take a hot-cross bun or bottle of pop to the fields or allotments down Water Eaton Road. It was a meeting-place for railwaymen. They'd share plants. Something you don't see now. There was real camaraderie.'

A concert party all dressed up for a performance of *The Mikado*, 1930s. The group is posing at the rear of Pacey's ironmonger's in Aylesbury Street, Fenny Stratford. The shop is now Pollard's and still an ironmonger's.

Winners of the fancy dress competition at the brickworks sports day, 1950. These events demonstrated the London Brick Company's philosophy of creating a family atmosphere among the workforce. This was a challenge, given the cosmopolitan mixture of Bletchley's growing population. But company chairman Sir Malcolm Stewart was an idealist.

Water not wind drove the majority of north Bucks mills. This is Water Eaton Mill, where children are enjoying the sight and sound of water running through the sluice gate, 1930s. Such big lads would not be seen in short trousers today! Martin Blane wore them until he left school at fourteen. 'Most kids had a big patch in their shorts and thought nothing of it. We used to swim in Water Eaton millpond. Some kids dived in and hurt themselves – it was only 4 ft deep. Because the water was always moving, it was always clean.'

Martin's brother, Donald Fraser, said: 'Life for children wasn't dull, though it was simpler than today's. Each child had to do certain chores in turn, such as sweeping the bricked yard, gathering food like dandelions and clover to feed the rabbits, which were kept in huts and killed for eating when grown. We kept chickens for eggs. The nest box for the broody hens was in the coal barn and we were careful not to disturb them. We were lucky if seven or eight chicks hatched. Other jobs for the boys included fetching groceries or meat and using a truck made from a grocer's sugar box to collect manure for the back garden. It meant getting up early in the morning and going along the roads most used by horses, shovelling up dung and bringing it home before we went to school.'

Jim White receives a bowling award from Mrs Hersee, wife of the brickworks manager, early 1950s. Jim was one of the first London Brick Company men to join Bletchley works after Read's was taken over. He remembers: 'Tommy Read was an old stager with his own way of doing things. Those [ways] were not right for London Brick. Ted Hersee was brought in as Tommy's assistant and almost immediately became manager. By that time Tommy was walking with a stick. He had to go.'

'Bubbles' Field, a London Brick Company maintenance bricklayer who cycled to work from Woburn, recalls training with this works tug-of-war team: 'We competed nationally and were among the best before the war. We used to pull against the old dumper loaded with brickbats.' Howard Beard was team coach and is sitting down giving advice.

Here the team compete at a local sports, 1950. I wonder what Howard Beard is saying. Baden Powell recounts what Howard said the day someone told him his house was on fire: 'Bloody good job. Tell 'em to throw a bit more on.' He didn't realize his leg wasn't being pulled.

Children enjoying Bletchley brickworks sports day, 1955. Their faces show delight in simple pleasures. Donald Fraser Blane recalls an age simpler still: 'Early spring would see boys, and sometimes girls, whipping tops along the roads, with only the occasional horse and cart to get in their way.'

The Second World War brought social upheaval and accelerated technology. Life became more complicated and faster. Accidents became more frequent and teams such as the Bletchley fire crew became more organized to deal with them. But even they have their delights; here they enjoy an old-fashioned 'cuppa' at Sherwood Drive, *c.* 1970.

Bletchley brickworks sports day, 1955. These events were familiar to me because my father was a lorry driver based at Bletchley brickyard. I remember refusing his command that I should take part in one of these little sprints and hiding behind a tree. It's a pity really, as it looks as if I missed a fair bit of fun!

Some years later I did at least repent my lack of athletic enthusiasm and joined Wolverton Athletic Club. Pounding the streets of Bletchley on a winter's night was part of my training schedule. Bletchley's illustrious youth record breaker, Ian Whittle, was sometimes among our training group striding through Fenny Stratford and along Whaddon Way.

'Thank heaven for little girls. They grow up in the most delightful ways.' This mum proudly displays her daughter for the camera at the brickworks sports day, 1950.

Seventeen-year-old Vanessa Harkness from Beanhill was crowned Bletchley Carnival Queen in June 1974. Receiving modelling offers as a result, she failed to return to Stantonbury Campus. Her worried mother feared she might be 'starstruck'. Headmaster Geoff Cooksey described Vanessa as a 'delightful girl at school' and was making enquiries as to where she might be.

Rock Solid pop group. Richard Lambourne, second from the left, is still going strong after years of rockin' and rollin'. He recalls playing to an audience of punks and skinheads at the Compass Club near the leisure centre, in 1983: 'It was crowded and smokey. These bikers arrived and a big fight started. We carried on playing.' Ann Gough, right, from Fenny Stratford, fronts his new group and keeps the audiences spellbound!

'The Battle of Bletchley', as the *Daily Express* called it. This was fun and games for some, when, in July 1966, objectors met government officials at Wilton Hall, Wilton Avenue, to protest that farmland would be lost and Bletchley would not be at the centre of the new city plan. Such gatherings were a far cry from Jenny Stacey's memories of Wilton Hall: 'We had dances there every week and top stars like The Rolling Stones, Johnny Kidd and Wayne Fontana. We used to hand our autograph books in at the stage door and collect them later. Dances stopped because of the fights. The rockers used to hang out in Greenway's Café, opposite W.H. Smith's.'

Here come the gentry, high on horseback and a delight to watch. In the words of a local poet: 'We're going to see the hunt today/A rip-roaring affair/Fine gents on horseback/Fine girls with golden hair.' Pictured here are the Whaddon Chasers, a historic hunt, riding towards Newton Longville, December 1970.

The Bull and Butcher pub, Aylesbury Street. A short way along this road, to the right of the picture, was Golding's shop. Mr Golding, a short, stumpy and dour-faced man, was popular for his ice-cream, made to his own recipe. He travelled by motor bike and sidecar all around the district selling his cornets and wafers, up until the 1940s. His popular recipe died with him.

Bletchley Water Buffalos (The Buffs), 1950s. Most of these men worked for the London Brick Company.

This late 1950s view shows the result of seventy years of in-filling. The New Inn used to stand in the centre right, but was replaced by The Bletchley Arms. The New Inn was a historic landmark indicating where Bletchley and Fenny Stratford parishes met, and was therefore known as 'Halfway House'. The white building next to The Bletchley Arms is the Studio cinema, which was opened in October 1936 by C.D. Flack JP, Chairman of Bletchley UDC. The first film shown there was *Mr Deeds Goes to Town*, starring Gary Cooper and Jean Arthur. Eight years later H.A. Alderman informed the *Bletchley Gazette*: 'I would hazard the conjecture that much of the immorality and aimless (or purposeful) street walking among young people has a close connection to the "oversaturation" with the lewd and sentimental treatment of the sensual side of life portrayed by the films.'

Jim Marshall autographs one of his famous amplifiers for a Dutch group, 1980s. When Jim started making amplifier cabinets, using his woodworking and engineering skills, few manufacturers catered for more than the average lead guitarist. Jim met Ken Bran, an apprentice at EMI, and employed him as a service engineer. Bran started developments which led to the world-famous sound described as rough, hard and distorted.

No stranger to awards, here is Jim with Phil Collins. Guitarist Bert Weedon holds the microphone and Davy Kaye is on Jim's right. Looking back on his years of success, Jim says: 'It has a lot to do with my being able to work sixteen hours a day. I saw my father struggle.' Jim's various jobs included biscuit-maker, scrap metal yard merchant and driving a horse and cart. He had only one complete year of schooling because of illness.

Children in their Sunday best outside St Martin's Church, 1907. Donald Fraser Blane recalls what used to happen after morning Sunday School at the Mission Church: 'The children formed a double line and marched to St Martin's Church, Aylesbury Street. After afternoon Sunday School we would ramble along the canal towpath and skim pebbles on the water, or in springtime look for violets and birds' nests. There is no doubt that the decline of religion and church attendance is because few children attend Sunday School these days.'

Donkey rides at Bletchley brickworks sports day, 1953.

UNDER CONTROL

Bletchley Road, near the Bedford Street junction, 1920s. The Conservative Party opened

offices in a large house behind the trees on the right – perhaps to guard their interests.

Bletchley Park viewed from the air, 1927. The house was built in 1860 and comprises half-timbered gables, oriels and a large domed Edwardian bay window. When Jewish financier Sir Herbert Leon bought it, he commissioned extensions in 1883 and 1906. His baronetcy was a reward for services to the Liberal Party. He was a respected local MP and friend of party leader Lloyd George. Bletchley Park was one of several large estates in the area and was symbolic of the social order. At least there was an order in those 'good old days'. Evidence suggests that most people were contented with their lot, even though health care was not so refined, and childhood was hazardous. People paid into sickness clubs to cover expenses.

Roly Doggett was named after Dr Roland Reynolds, who died quite young. 'In my youth we went to Dr Maddison, before and during the war. The elderly Dorothy Lovekin took over while he was called up. She was a tweedy woman with thick brown stockings. We had a scarlet-fever outbreak in 1946 and the house had to be fumigated.' Roly spent his schooldays under the influence of E.C. Cook: 'He rolled his "r"s and used to whack us at times, but that was understandable. He was a disciplinarian. If you were late in when the whistle blew, you were marched straight into Billy Bennett's workshop. No excuse. Whack!'

There were no serious social excusers or excuses. Discipline was tough, but Lady Fanny Leon exercised a charitable hand after her husband's death in 1926. Sir Herbert was known to have complained about the sound of St Mary's Church bells and the noisy steam engines, both close to his home. He was also unsympathetic to suffragettes, but overall he had a beneficial effect on Bletchley. The bells were silenced for his funeral and men stopped and doffed their hats. Lady Fanny continued her good works until her death in 1937.

Captain Faulkner's property consortium bought the park but war clouds thwarted his residential development scheme. The Foreign Office needed a quiet country home for a cypher school and the park was ideal, being situated on a good rail link to London and connecting Oxford and Cambridge. The park was about to become a legend worth fighting for – though it was something of a struggle for a dedicated group of locals to get the place preserved as an active museum site in the 1990s. The developers were after it again. (Huntingdon Aero Films)

This group includes Sidney Rowland (left), his mother Mrs Thomas Rowland and Revd Mr Jones, *c*. 1900. The Rowlands were Fenny Stratford timber merchants and landlords to Donald Fraser Blane's parents. Donald used to take his family's handcart to the Rowland's sawmill in Simpson Road to collect firewood. The timber was stacked along the verges to season over the years and was delivered on big wagons pulled by horses or steam engines.

Posing for the family portrait used to be a serious business. This one shows George Cheshire, a pastry cook of 41 High Street, Fenny Stratford, with his eight children, *c*. 1912.

The Baptist church (formerly known as the Spurgeon Memorial Church) in Fenny Stratford was built in 1892 and stood in Aylesbury Street, at the opposite end to St Martin's Church. Golding's shop is the second building to the right of the Baptist church. A garage has replaced the thatched cottages.

St Margaret's Mission Hall, at the top of Brooklands Road, was a sister church to St Martin's and was known as 'the Mission'. Martin Blane recalls that he spent his Sundays singing in the Mission choir. 'We got paid a penny, which was good.'

Noel Cottages, Church Green Road. They were built for Sir Herbert Leon's servants in 1904.

The President of the Baptist Union outside the chapel, 1906.

Old Bletchley parish started west of the railway bridge, and its established church was St Mary's. This picture was taken in the 1930s and show the tall poplars and fine yews leading up to the Norman porch and great doorway. English builders pointed the round Norman arch, retaining the beak moulding and heads of Norman patricians and Saxon peasants. All was bright and beautiful, including the church's fortress-like battlements.

St Martin's Church, over the boundary in Fenny Stratford, on the Aylesbury/Watling Street crossroads, *c*. 1911. Antiquarian Browne Willis was the lord of the manor who inspired this Gothic masterpiece, and local subscriptions and Oxbridge colleges helped to fund it. Begun in 1724, it was consecrated five years later.

The interior of the church, *c*. 1911. A south aisle had been added in 1823, doubling its size. John Chadwick, urban council surveyor, built a new south aisle and added the organ chamber in 1908. The moulded arches are on circular reddish sandstone piers and open on to the Willis Chapel. There is a tombstone to Browne Willis, who died at Whaddon in 1760, relatively poor after doing much to benefit the county's churches.

Staple Hall, Fenny Stratford, under occupation by the military during the First World War. Huts were built in the grounds for the common soldier. After the war, one of these was sold and transported to Simpson parish, 2 miles north, for use as a village hall. Robert Maxwell addressed election meetings there in the 1960s during his campaigns for parliament.

Father Cyril Wheeler fires the first Fenny popper, on a St Martin's Day between the wars. The popper was created by putting a gunpowder charge into a metal cylinder and then inserting a red hot poker. The purpose was to salute Browne Willis, whose idea it had been to salute St Martin on St Martin's Day. This was a tradition for over 250 years, but an uncontrolled explosion in 1949 broke glass in the church clock, signalling that it was time to move this curious practice to Leon Recreation Ground.

Proper social control started in school, under the firm guidance of ladies like Mrs Edwards, a schoolteacher at Bletchley Road Leon School. She is pictured here during the First World War.

Children, parents and staff at Newton Longville village school, 2 miles south of Bletchley, early 1950s. Midge Day recalls: 'It was lovely growing up in Newton Longville. Everybody knew everybody else and used to help each other. It was always busy with brick lorries and the baker's van came round. But we could skip, and play hopscotch and marbles in the street.'

Those who lament this age of unisex clothes and jogging suits might well reflect that in olden times folk knew their place and usually dressed the part. Here is Mrs Will Norman, who walked 3 miles to her wedding in the spring sunshine in 1905. She earned the distinction of being the first person to lead a cow into the new Bletchley market when it was transferred from Fenny Stratford in 1924.

Her husband, Will 'Drover' Norman, used to drive the beasts all over Bucks. He suffered a badly gored shoulder but that did not stop him. One of his few indulgences was to call on Winslow barber Bill Small for a fortnightly shave with a cut-throat razor.

Bill Day, right, with two other boys being looked after at Miss Jones's home near Newton Longville, mid-1920s.

Bill (husband of Midge Day; see p. 63) is pictured here just before his departure to Singapore. He was captured by the Japanese and spent 3½ years half starved and building the Burma railway, famed for its bridge over the River Kwai. Bert Viccars was a fellow Bletchley brickworker who suffered inhuman treatment at the hands of Japanese 'warriors'.

Special Constable Thomas Marchant patrolling Bedford Street, 1940. In those days there was less visible crime and relatively few assaults on the person. However, Mr Marchant was endeavouring to protect a community under serious threat from an outside enemy, Germany. In this connection, one mother informed the *Bletchley Gazette* in February 1943 that Mr Burridge, Rector of Bletchley, was misguided in urging people to think kindly of the Germans: 'I am not alone in my hate of the German race. Millions share it. This vile race caused the last war and this. Our fathers and sons answered the call to protect us, but Mr Burridge refused to stand with them.'

The former Fenny Stratford police station, Simpson Road, 1994. Rendered surplus to requirements by the new headquarters in Sherwood Drive, the building has long since exchanged a role with the more obvious forces of law and order for one with social services. Baden Powell reported here during the war to sign up with the Local Defence Volunteers (LDV – often construed as Look, Duck and Vanish), better known as the Home Guard. 'Three of us went down. There was a cubby-hole just inside the door. This big old sergeant opened it and said, "What do you want?" We told him and had to register our names. First one goes up and says "Baden King", then the other "Baden Bates". Gets to me and he says "I suppose you're bloomin' Baden Powell." "Yes," I said.'

Wrens were among hundreds of service personnel billeted in the area to work at Bletchley Park. Decoding enemy messages encoded by the German Enigma and Lorenz machines proved quite a task before these 1,500 valve Colossus computers were employed. The park had its own electricity supply and Baden Powell was one of the men looking after it. 'We were always on standby. Mine was a reserved occupation.'

GI bride Pat Dobbs met American serviceman Layle Kellogg while working as a civil service typist in Bletchley during the war. 'Layle was a dog handler. We would meet for dates outside the post office and go to a film at the Studio cinema opposite. My parents were upset when I said I wanted to marry him and settle in the USA. I was their only child. My dad was a cobbler. He wouldn't have the money to visit me very often. I was young. It was a very big step.'

Mavis Dyson (née Byford), left, with other station staff at Bletchley, 1942. 'It was very sad seeing all the coffins being loaded on trains. They were for the young servicemen killed in training exercises at local airfields.'

Riding with this well-poised Whaddon Chase hunt has always been a mark of social standing. In the 1920s the hunt was proud to count the Prince of Wales among its number. However, between 1924 and 1928 there were a number of incidents involving brothers Syd and Bert Illing, who farmed at Salden, on the Buckingham side of Bletchley. These reached a climax when Syd spoke roughly to the Prince of Wales and fired his shotgun. The fox which the hunters were chasing mysteriously disappeared. This picture shows the hunt strolling through Bletchley brickworks, December 1970.

Firefighting equipment had come a long way by the 1920s and though immaculately turned out, this horse-drawn steam pump was getting a bit long in the tooth. These horses belonged to the local council. If they were pulling the dustcart when the siren sounded, they would be unhitched and galloped to the fire station. The firemen pictured are, left to right: Frank Howard (captain), Bert Nix (driver), Will Busler, Will Clarke, Jack Day, Frank Tattam, John Brooks (who succeeded Frank Howard as captain), Eric Matthews, Ern French.

This Renault lorry came into service in about 1932 and was used to tow a Merryweather steam pump. It was easier than having to catch the horses and could travel faster – until it was faced with a muddy farm track and became bogged down. Here the men and machines are outside Leon School, Bletchley Road.

Bletchley fire pumps and crews pose outside Sherwood Drive fire station, 18 February 1969. The new station included the town's nuclear fall-out shelter, behind a lead door to the basement. Firefighter Colin Matthew observed: 'Its weakness was revealed when we washed our cars outside and water leaked down into it through a grating.'

The fire station was still very new at this open day in the 1960s, but the fire engine was not. Remarkably, Colin Matthew recalls travelling from the old Church Street premises to incidents on the M1 motorway shortly after it opened in 1959. This machine was affectionately called Elizabeth, on account of the number plate. Following its withdrawal, it was given to White Spires School for children to play on.

A proud moment for PC Alan Turvey, left, of Bletchley traffic division at Buckingham Sub-Division Police Recreation Club's annual dinner, held at Stowe School. Chief Constable Brigadier J.H. Cheney is presenting him with the Rothschild Cup for the most gallant act of 1963. PC Turvey was called to the M1 service station at Newport Pagnell, where he was kicked and trodden on but still managed to contain six hooligans until reinforcements arrived.

Labour Home Secretary David Hennels visiting Sherwood Way fire station, 1969. Station Officer Greaves stands to his left. Colin Matthew remembers a certain amount of tension in the 1960s between local part-timers and newcomers, many ex-servicemen, coming in as full-timers and taking over most of the 'shouts'. More change came after the 1977 strike. Colin remarked: 'People brought us wood for our fires as we sat picketing outside the station. They supported us. We went from a 56-hour week to 42 hours and got a 30 per cent pay rise.'

Terrapin International is a mainstay of the local economy, selling and renting out pre-engineered building systems. This picture shows a fire at its Bletchley premises on 21 June 1968.

Firemen dealing with a blaze at the Lakes estate, mid-1960s. These system-built houses were a quick solution to a severe housing shortage. In 1965 the *Chronicle and Echo* reported that 'it was all very well bringing more and more people to the town from London – but by now the second generation was growing up and getting married. They needed houses of their own.'

Voluntary activity has always been vital to meeting needs missed by the authorities which are supposed to be in control. Here Bletchley firemen do their bit, early 1970s. They built this mini replica of a fire engine and pushed it to Lambeth, to raise money for children's charities.

The St John Ambulance Brigade attended Simpson Church to dedicate its first motor ambulance, shown here. The nursing section was founded in 1930. The brigade moved to Bletchley Road during the war and in 1944 the *Bletchley Gazette* reported: 'An attempt was being made to coordinate ambulance services in the region. It is not an easy problem, for it means that separate ambulance-owning authorities must agree to pool their services to a greater extent than they do now.'

The ambulance service came under county control after the war, though Bletchley's St John Brigade continued its voluntary activities from a new base in Sherwood Way. This picture shows the professionals attending a road accident in the early 1970s. There was still no local hospital and it was a long drive to the casualty department.

Crime is an increasing threat to order, and unemployment seems to encourage it. But much crime goes beyond being a means of survival. The Great Train Robbery was a dash for riches. It took place on a bridge a few miles south of Bletchley, on 8 August 1963. The captured robbers were taken to Linslade police station, shown here, where the newshounds gathered.

A Panda patrol in Queensway, on the long night of 31 August 1973. PC Derek Edwards is on the lookout for trouble. Incidents included a bomb scare in The Dolphin pub, a fight at Water Eaton Coronation Hall and a noisy party on the Lakes estate. It was one thing after another. The struggle goes on to keep matters under control.

Acknowledgements

Many people have helped me to assemble this collection and to give it life through the captions. There is not room to explain their various contributions in any detail. I can only say that they were all very important. I hope this book does them justice. They are listed below in alphabetical order. Every reasonable effort has been made to trace photograph copyright holders.

Ray Akins • D. Barrow • Ken Barrow • Bill Barton • Fred Bateman
Tom Bates • Ray Bellchambers • Donald Fraser Blane • Gwen Blane
Martin Blane • Bletchley Archaeological and Historical Society
Jack Bromfield • Ruth Bromfield • B. Brooksbank
Bucks County Fire and Rescue
Bucks County Library – Julian Hunt and Jane Cutler • *Bucks Herald*
Midge Day • Pat Dobbs • Roland Doggett • Mavis Dyson • Bubbles Field
Annie Freeman • Cyril Freeman • Jeffrey Goddard • Albert Hughes
H.L. Holland • Huntingdon Aero Films • Olive Knapp • Reg Knapp
Richard Lambourne • Jim Marshall • Marshall Amplification
Colin Matthew • Bob North • Baden Powell • D. Shepherd • Colin Stacey
Jenny Stacey • Stantonbury Campus • Roy Stockham • Thames Valley Police
Des Tunks • Bert Viccars • Jim White

Finally, thanks to my wife, Nicola, who wishes me to point out that she shared my brief experience as a Bletchley market trader, suffering the perishing winds at the end of Queensway, in the pursuit of a fortune we never made!

BRITAIN IN OLD PHOTOGRAPHS

To order any of these titles please telephone Littlehampton Book Services on 01903 721596